To <u>Laura - A Great Mom</u>

From <u>Uncle John & Aunt Betty</u>

Date <u>Sunday 8th May 2011</u>

365 Things Every Mother Should Know

© 2005 Christian Art Gifts, RSA
        Christian Art Gifts Inc., IL, USA

First edition © 2005
Second edition © 2010

Compiled by Wilma le Roux and Lynette Douglas

Designed by Christian Art Gifts
Images used under license from Shutterstock.com

Printed in China

ISBN 978-1-77036-555-1

10 11 12 13 14 15 16 17 18 19 – 10 9 8 7 6 5 4 3 2 1

365 things every
MOTHER
should know

Contents

Foreword

Being a mother is one of a woman's highest callings. In this God-given role, she influences the world and the future, she prepares the hearts of children for eternity. Time spent with children is never wasted. It resounds to the far corners of the earth and reverberates to the farthest reaches of heaven. This little book provides you with 365 inspiring quotes and thoughts – some sublime, some light-hearted – that will encourage you in your great work.

A Mother's Words

1.

I think the one lesson
I have learned is that
there is no substitute
for paying attention.

Diane Sawyer

2.

The language of love is
spoken with a look,
a touch, a sigh, a kiss, and
sometimes a word.

Frank Tyger

3.

Kind words are jewels that
live in the heart and soul
and remain as blessed memories
years after they have been spoken.

Marvea Johnson

4.

The most important thing in
communication is to hear
what isn't being said.

Peter F. Drucker

5.

All the beautiful sentiments
in the world weigh less than
a single lovely action.

James Russell Lowell

6.

The art of conversation
lies in listening.

Malcolm Forbes

7.

Whatever is in your heart
determines what you say.

Luke 6:45 NLT

8.

A word aptly spoken is like apples
of gold in settings of silver.

Proverbs 25:11

9.

I think there is something
wonderful about everyone,
and whenever I get the
opportunity to tell
someone this, I do.

Mary Kay

10.

Don't expect others to
listen to your advice and
ignore your example.
someone this, I do.

H. Jackson Brown, Jr.

11.

In times like the present,
men should utter nothing
for which they would not
willingly be responsible through
time and in eternity.

Abraham Lincoln

12.

My dear brothers, take
note of this: Everyone should be
quick to listen, slow to speak
and slow to become angry.

James 1:19

13.

A mother is someone who dreams for you,
but then lets you chase the dreams you have
for yourself and loves you just the same.

14.

Silence is a great peacemaker.

Henry Wadsworth Longfellow

15.

A dining room
table with children's eager,
hungry faces around it, ceases to
be a mere dining room
table and becomes an altar.

Simeon Strunsky

16.

One of the best ways to
persuade others is with your
ears – by listening to them.

Dean Rusk

17.

Anything will give up its
secrets if you love it enough.

George Washington Carver

18.

The real art of conversation
is not only to say the right thing
at the right place, but to leave unsaid
the wrong thing at the tempting moment.

Dorothy Nevill

19.

Kind words can be short and easy to
speak, but their echoes are truly endless.

Mother Teresa

20.

"No" is always a door-closing word;
"Yes" is a door-opening word.

Thomas Dreier

21.

The little things are most worthwhile –
a quiet word, a look, a smile.

Margaret Lindsey

22.

Little deeds of kindness,
little words of love.
Make our earth an Eden,
like the heaven above.

Julia Fletcher Carney

23.

Worry weighs a person down;
an encouraging word
cheers a person up.

Proverbs 12:25 NLT

24.

Encouragement is
oxygen to the soul.

George M. Adams

25.

A mother understands
what a child does not say.

Proverb

26.

Listen, my son, to your father's
instruction and do not forsake your
mother's teaching. They will be
a garland to grace your head
and a chain to adorn your neck.

Proverbs 1:8-9

The Love of a Mother

27.

The one who truly loves gives
all and sacrifices nothing.

Rainer Maria Rilke

28.

Love covers over all wrongs.

Proverbs 10:12

29.

Give a little love to a child
and you get a great deal back.

John Ruskin

30.

The way to love someone is to lightly
run your finger over that person's soul
until you find a crack, and then gently
pour your love into that crack.

Keith Miller

31.

A kiss is a rosy dot over the "i" of loving.

Cyrano de Bergerac

32.

Compassion and mercy
warm the human soul like
sunshine and summer
breezes warm the human body.

James King

33.

Love always protects,
always trusts, always hopes,
always perseveres.

1 Corinthians 13:7

34.

I truly feel that there are as many
ways of loving as there are people
in the world and as there are days
in the lives of those people.

Mary Calderone

35.

No language can express the power
and beauty and heroism and majesty
of a mother's love. It shrinks not where
man cowers, and grows stronger where
man faints, and over the wastes of
worldly fortune sends the radiance of its
quenchless fidelity like a star in heaven.

E. H. Chapin

36.

The mother loves her child most divinely,
not when she surrounds him with
comfort and anticipates his wants,
but when she resolutely holds him
to the highest standards and is content
with nothing less than his best.

Hamilton Wright Mabie

37.

Parental love – the one
reliable antidote for life's pains.

Vance Packard

38.

Children don't care how
much you know, until
they know how much you care.

39.

The love of a mother is the
veil of a softer light between
the heart and the heavenly Father.

Samuel Taylor Coleridge

40.

A mother's love endures
through all; in good repute,
in bad repute, in the face of
the world's condemnation, a
mother still loves on.

Washington Irving

41.

A child needs your love most
when he deserves it least.

Erma Bombeck

42.

The father is the head
of the home, but the
mother is the heart of the home.

43.

Mother is the sweetest word that ever one
could say: It speaks of love and tenderness,
and quiet beauty day by day.

44.

Faith is the strength and
courage God gives you to
help you to fill each day with
words and deeds of love.

Louisa May Alcott's mother

45.

In a mother's arms there is shelter
from the storms of life; peace
when the heart is troubled; joy when
the day is dark. Her love never fails.

46.

Kids go where there's excitement.
They stay where there's love.

Zig Ziglar

47.

Mother means selfless devotion,
limitless sacrifice, and
love that passes understanding.

48.

A mother's love is a beacon light
that shines faith, and truth, and prayer;
and through the changing scenes of
life, her children find a haven there.

49.

In the midst of everything,
mothers should take time
to love and laugh and pray.
Then life will be worth living,
each and every day.

Susan Wall

A Mother's Laughter

50.

Rejoice in the Lord always.
I will say it again: Rejoice!

Philippians 4:4

51.

A good laugh makes us
better friends with ourselves
and everybody around us.

Orison Swett Marden

52.

Sarah said, "God has brought
me laughter, and everyone who
hears about this will laugh with me."

Genesis 21:6

53.

Humor is the great thing, the saving thing.
The minute it crops up, all our irritations
and resentments flit away, and a sunny
spirit takes their place.

Mark Twain

54.

Whole-hearted, ready laughter heals,
encourages, relaxes anyone within hearing
distance. The laughter that springs from
love makes wide the space around –
gives room for the loved one to enter in.

Eugenia Price

55.

A cheerful heart is
good medicine, but a crushed
spirit dries up the bones.

Proverbs 17:22

56.

Our mouths were filled with laughter,
our tongues with songs of joy. Then it was
said among the nations, "The LORD has
done great things for them."

Psalm 126:2

57.

A happy heart makes the face cheerful.

Proverbs 15:13

58.

People who laugh actually live
longer than those who don't laugh.
Few persons realize that health
actually varies according to
the amount of laughter.

James Walsh

59.

He will yet fill your mouth
with laughter and your lips
with shouts of joy.

Job 8:21

60.

Laughter is the hand of God
on the shoulder of a troubled world.

Grady Nutt

61.

Advice is sometimes transmitted
more successfully through a
joke than grave teaching.

Baltasar Gracián

62.

Mirth is God's medicine.

Henry Ward Beecher

63.

The most wasted day is that in
which we have not laughed.

Nicolas Chamfort

64.

One filled with joy preaches
without preaching.

Mother Teresa

65.

Jesus fills with life, love, and laughter
each heart that opens like a flower
to the sunshine of His love.

66.

God fills our lives with blessings
that fill our hearts with joy.

67.

You have filled my heart with
greater joy than when their
grain and new wine abound.

Psalm 4:7

68.

Laughter is the most beautiful
and beneficial therapy God
ever granted humanity.

Charles Swindoll

69.

A joyful heart is like the sunshine of
God's love, the hope of eternal happiness.

Mother Teresa

70.

You have made known to me the path of life;
You will fill me with joy in Your presence, with
eternal pleasures at Your right hand.

Psalm 16:11

A Mother's Comfort

71.

Mother – that was the bank where
we deposited all our hurts and worries.

T. De Witt Talmage

72.

And we know that in all things God works for
the good of those who love Him, who have
been called according to His purpose.

Romans 8:28

73.

Today, whatever may annoy, the
word for me is joy, simple joy.

John Kendrick Bangs

74.

Once upon a memory, someone wiped
away a tear, held me close and loved me.
Thank you, Mother dear.

75.

It is difficult to give children a sense
of security unless you have it yourself.
If you have it, they catch it from you.

William C. Menninger

76.

But the Lord is faithful, and He
will strengthen and protect
you from the evil one.

2 Thessalonians 3:3

77.

Be not perplexed, be not afraid,
everything passes, God does not change.
Patience wins all things, he who has God
lacks nothing; God alone suffices.

Teresa of Avila

78.

You must live with people
to know their problems,
and live with God in
order to solve them.

P. T. Forsyth

79.

The LORD is my rock, my fortress
and my deliverer; my God is my rock, in
whom I take refuge. He is my shield and
the horn of my salvation, my stronghold.

Psalm 18:2

80.

What you need to know
when you're tempted
to jump into your kids' troubles
with both feet, you're not the
trouble-fixer. God is.

Barbara Johnson

81.

Nobody said life would be perfect.
Nobody said your kids would go through
life scot-free of troubles. But what
your kids need to know is that God
can be trusted to never leave, no matter
how hot the trouble gets.

Barbara Johnson

82.

We could never learn to be brave and patient, if there were only joy in the world.

Helen Keller

83.

And the peace of God, which transcends all understanding, will guard your hearts and your minds in Christ Jesus.

Philippians 4:7

84.

If you hem in both ends of your day with a prayer, it won't be so likely to unravel in the middle.

Thomas F. Shubnell

85.

A surrendered life was what Mother modeled for us. When life knocked her to her knees, she learned that was the best position for prayer.

June Hunt

86.

For in the day of trouble He will
keep me safe in His dwelling; He will
hide me in the shelter of His tabernacle
and set me high upon a rock.

Psalm 27:5

87.

Every day, commit the ones you love
unto God's care and keeping. It's the
best – and the only – thing you can do.

Family Life

88.

There can be no rainbow
without a cloud and a storm.

John H. Vincent

Wealth and Riches

89.

The best-paid job in the world
is to be a full-time mother.
The wages are always pure love.

Mildred Vermont

90.

Ask thy purse what thou shouldst spend.

Elizabeth Stone

91.

It isn't the big pleasures that count the most;
it's making a great deal out of the little ones.

Jean Webster

92.

But remember the LORD your God, for it is
He who gives you the ability to produce
wealth, and so confirms His covenant, which
He swore to your forefathers, as it is today.

Deuteronomy 8:18

93.

Whoever trusts in his riches
will fall, but the righteous will
thrive like a green leaf.

Proverbs 11:28

94.

The habit of saving is itself an education;
it fosters every virtue, teaches self-denial,
cultivates the sense of order, trains to
forethought, and so broadens the mind.

Theodore T. Munger

95.

Let's not get so busy or live so fast
that we can't listen to the music of the
meadow or the symphony that glorifies
the forest. Some things in the world are
far more important than wealth; one of
them is the ability to enjoy simple things.

Dale Carnegie

96.

If you want to feel rich,
just count all the things you
have that money can't buy.

97.

Not what we have but what we
enjoy, constitutes our abundance.

John Senn

98.

I was young and now I am old, yet I
have never seen the righteous forsaken
or their children begging bread. They are
always generous and lend freely;
their children will be blessed.

Psalm 37:25-26

99.

I am indeed rich, since my
income is superior to my expense,
and my expense is equal to my wishes.

Edward Gibbon

100.

It's good to have money and the things
that money can buy, but it's good, too,
to check up once in a while and make
sure that you haven't lost the things
that money can't buy.

George Horace Lorimer

101.

But godliness with contentment is great gain. For we brought nothing into the world, and we can take nothing out of it. But if we have food and clothing, we will be content with that. People who want to get rich fall into temptation and a trap and into many foolish and harmful desires that plunge men into ruin and destruction.

1 Timothy 6:6-9

102.

It's not what you'd do with a million, if riches should e'er be your lot, but what are you doing at present with the dollar and a quarter you've got?

103.

Honor the LORD with your wealth, with the firstfruits of all your crops; then your barns will be filled to overflowing, and your vats will brim over with new wine.

Proverbs 3:9-10

104.

Filling a child's room with
games and toys and designer clothes
can never fill his heart with love.

105.

Keep your lives free from the love of
money and be content with what you
have, because God has said, "Never will
I leave you; never will I forsake you."

Hebrews 13:5

106.

A cheerful giver does not count
the cost of what he gives.
His heart is set on pleasing and
cheering him to whom the gift is given.

Julian of Norwich

107.

Command those who are rich in this
present world not to be arrogant nor
to put their hope in wealth, which
is so uncertain, but to put their hope
in God, who richly provides us
with everything for our enjoyment.

1 Timothy 6:17

108.

There is a vast difference in some instances
between what we really need and that
which we think we must have, and the
realization of this truth will greatly lessen
the seeming discomfort of doing without.

William Peck

109.

"So do not worry, saying, 'What shall we eat?'
or 'What shall we drink?' or 'What shall
we wear?' For the pagans run after all these
things, and your heavenly Father knows
that you need them. But seek first His
kingdom and His righteousness, and all
these things will be given to you as well."

Matthew 6:31-33

Growing Up

110.

Your children are grown
up when they stop asking
you where they came
from and refuse to tell you
where they are going.

P. J. O'Rourke

111.

There are only two lasting
bequests we can give to our children.
One is roots; the other, wings.

Hodding Carter

112.

And the child grew and
became strong; He was filled
with wisdom, and the grace
of God was upon Him.

Luke 2:40

113.

The instruction received
at a mother's knee is never
quite effaced from the soul.

Lamennais

114.

Let your children go if you
want to keep them.

Malcolm Forbes

115.

Avoid pressing problems.
Wash and dry children's clothes
and leave them in the ironing
basket until the kids outgrow them.

Peggy Goldtrap

116.

Cleaning the house while your
kids are still growing is like shoveling
the walk before it stops snowing.

Phyllis Diller

117.

Elderly people and those in
authority cannot always be
relied upon to take enlightened and
comprehending views of what they
call the indiscretions of youth.

Winston Churchill

118.

If society is to preserve
stability and a degree of
continuity, it must know how to
keep its adolescents from imposing
their tastes, attitudes, values, and
fantasies on everyday life.

Eric Hoffer

119.

Youth is a frightening age ...
so many problems; so little
wisdom to solve them.

Walter Hoving

120.

Youth is the opportunity to do
something and become somebody.

Theodore Munger

121.

Like its politicians and its wars,
society has the teenagers it deserves.

J. B. Priestly

122.

Remember that as a teenager
you are in the last stage of your
life when you will be happy
to hear the phone is for you.

Frank Tyger

123.

Train a child in the
way he should go, and
when he is old he
will not turn from it.

Proverbs 22:6

124.

A child is a person who is going to
carry on what you have started …
the fate of humanity is in his hands.

Abraham Lincoln

125.

Adolescence is the
period of life when
we first become obsessed
with trying to prove we
are not a child – an obsession
that can last a lifetime.

Cullen Hightower

126.

There's a time – all too brief
as it soon becomes apparent to parents –
to be little; a time to be in between;
and a time to be old. Let each have its
season … Let the little be little.

Malcolm Forbes

127.

How soon do we forget what
elders used to know:
that children should be raised,
not left like weeds to grow.

Art Buck

128.

When I was a child, I talked like
a child, I thought like a child,
I reasoned like a child.
When I became a man,
I put childish ways behind me.

1 Corinthians 13:11

129.

Every adult should be an
expert on teenagers,
after spending life's seven
longest years being one.

Cullen Hightower

130.

Nothing you do for your
children is ever wasted.
They seem not to notice us,
hovering, averting our eyes,
and they seldom offer thanks,
but what we do for them is never wasted.

Garrison Keillor

131.

In the final analysis it is not what you have
done for your children but what you have taught
them to do for themselves that will make them
successful human beings.

Ann Landers

132.

Teenagers are people who
express a burning desire to be
different by dressing exactly alike.

133.

The parent's job year in and year
out, here a little, there a little, is to build
up a disposition of good sportsmanship,
of taking one's medicine, of facing the
music, of being reviled and reviling not.

Samuel Smith Drury

134.

And He said: "I tell you the truth,
unless you change and become
like little children, you will never
enter the kingdom of heaven.
Therefore, whoever humbles
himself like this child is the greatest
in the kingdom of heaven. And
whoever welcomes a little child
like this in My name welcomes Me."

Matthew 18:3-5

Home, Sweet Home

135.

Houses are made of wood and
stone, but only love can make a home.

136.

Nothing can compare in beauty, and
wonder, and admirableness, and divinity
itself, to the silent work in obscure
dwellings of faithful women bringing their
children to honor and virtue and piety.

Henry Ward Beecher

137.

Enjoy one another and take the
time to enjoy family life together.
Quality time is no substitute for quantity
time. Quantity time is quality time.

Billy Graham

138.

In the 25 years that I have practiced
psychiatry, I have never come across a child
with serious emotional problems whose parents
love each other and whose love for their child is
an outflowing of their love for each other.

Justin Green

139.

What is a home? It is the laughter
of a child, the song of a mother
and the strength of a father.

Ernestine Schumann-Heink

140.

The best things are the simplest things,
home and love and work to do …
flowers in the garden and bread from
the generous fields. Lacking these, what else
can make life worth the living? Having them,
give thanks with joy; we need no more.

141.

Home is the magic circle within which
the weary spirit finds refuge; it is the sacred
asylum to which the care worn heart retreats
to find rest from all the toils and cares of life.
Home! That name touches every fiber of our
soul. And as dear as home can be is the mother
that presided over it, and that we loved.

Mary G. Clarke

142.

A baby enters your home and makes
so much noise for twenty years you can
hardly stand it – then departs, leaving the
house so silent you think you'll go mad.

J. A. Holmes

143.

Good family life is never an accident but always
an achievement by those who share it.

James H. S. Bossard

144.

Happy are families where the government of
parents is the reign of affection, and obedience
of the children the submission of love.

Francis Bacon

145.

Where there is a mother
in the house, matters speed well.

Amos Bronson Alcott

146.

A child was asked, "Where is your home?"
Looking up with loving eyes at his mother,
he replied, "Where mother is."

147.

By the time the youngest children have
learned to keep the house tidy, the oldest
grandchildren are on hand to tear it to pieces.

Christopher Morley

148.

The home is a lighthouse which has the
lamp of God on the table and the light of
Christ in the window, to give guidance to
those who wander in darkness.

Henry Rische

149.

A child's home is his first school and the first
church where he learns of a loving God.

Ernestine Schumann-Heink

150.

The crown of the house is godliness.
The beauty of the house is order.
The glory of the house is hospitality.
The blessing of the house is contentment.

151.

A home is the total contribution of love
on the part of each one dwelling within it.

Anne Pannell

152.

If this world affords true happiness, it is to be
found in a home where love and confidence
increase with years, where the necessities
of life come without severe strain, where
luxuries enter only after their cost
has been carefully considered.

A. Edward Newton

153.

Govern a family as you would
cook a small fish – very gently.

Chinese proverb

154.

Every house where love abides and
friendship is a guest, is surely home, and home,
sweet home; for there the heart can rest.

Henry van Dyke

155.

This is the true nature of home –
it is the place of peace; the shelter,
not only from injury, but from
all terror, doubt, and division.

John Ruskin

156.

By wisdom a house is built, and
through understanding it is established.

Proverbs 24:3

A Mother's Faith

157.

There is no higher height to
which humanity can attain than
that occupied by a devoted,
heaven-inspired, praying mother.

158.

How important it is to teach children
not only to present their requests to
God, but also to thank and praise
Him for who He is and for all His answers!
By doing so you are cultivating a grateful
heart – one that will more likely be
open to a relationship with the Father.

Annie Datton

159.

Pray together with your children in
honest terms that are appropriate to
their age and understanding. Then daily
trust God to do His work in all of you.

Carole Streeter

160.

In my opinion, what we need to
teach children is that prayer is friendly
conversation, frequently conversing alone,
with One whom we know loves us.

Teresa of Avila

161.

The real religion of the world comes from
women – from mothers most of all, who
carry the key of our souls in their bosoms.

Oliver Wendall Holmes

162.

Pray together and read the Bible together.
Nothing strengthens a marriage and family more.
Nothing is better defense against Satan.

Billy Graham

163.

"The family that prays together, stays
together" is much more than a cliché!
And when the family adds the dimension
of praying together in church, the truth
becomes even stronger.

Zig Ziglar

164.

God is continually drawing us to
Himself in everything we experience.

Gerard Hughes

165.

Once you become aware that
the main business you are here for
is to know God, most of life's problems
fall into place of their own accord.

J. I. Packer

166.

Love of God purifies and
ennobles every taste and desire,
intensifies every affection,
and brightens every worthy pleasure.

167.

Jesus answered, "It is written:
'Man does not live on bread alone,
but on every word that comes
from the mouth of God.'"

Matthew 4:4

168.

The only way a parent can teach children
to love God with all their passion and
commitment, with all their being and intellect,
with all their energy and stamina – is for that
truth to come from what the parent
truly is in his or her own heart.

Gloria Gaither

169.

The Light of God surrounds me.
The Love of God enfolds me.
The Power of God protects me.
The Presence of God watches over me.
Wherever I am, God is.

Catherine Marshall

170.

Every moment of life is spent in the sight and
company of an omniscient, omnipresent Creator.

J. I. Packer

171.

Lord, what a change within us one short hour
spent in Thy presence will avail to make!

Richard Trench

172.

"Be still, and know that I am
God; I will be exalted among the
nations, I will be exalted in the earth."

Psalm 46:10

173.

Oh, the loving strength that
surges from His heart to yours all day;
like a bright and shining armor, just
because you knelt to pray!

Alice Mortenson

174.

Jesus, Son of human mother, bless
our motherhood we pray; give us
grace to lead our children, draw
them to Thee day by day.

Emily Shirreff

175.

Study to shew thyself approved
unto God, a workman that
needeth not to be ashamed,
rightly dividing the word of truth.

2 Timothy 2:15 KJV

176.

Walk so close to God that
nothing can come between you.

177.

I have no greater joy than to hear
that my children are walking in the truth.

3 John 4

178.

But grow in the grace
and knowledge of our Lord and
Savior Jesus Christ. To Him be glory
both now and forever. Amen.

2 Peter 3:18

179.

The love of the Father is like
a sudden rain shower that will pour
forth when you least expect it, catching
you up into wonder and praise.

Richard J. Foster

180.

Finally, brethren, whatsoever things
are true, whatsoever things are honest,
whatsoever things are just, whatsoever
things are pure, whatsoever things
are lovely, whatsoever things are of
good report; if there be any virtue, and if
there be any praise, think on these things.

Philippians 4:8 KJV

181.

To love God is the greatest of all virtues;
to be loved by God is the greatest of blessings.

Portuguese proverb

182.

All the troubles of life come upon
us because we refuse to sit quietly
for a while each day in our rooms.

Blaise Pascal

183.

And thou shalt love the Lord thy
God with all thy heart, and with all thy
soul, and with all thy mind, and with all thy
strength: this is the first commandment.

Mark 12:30 KJV

Nurturing

184.

The formative period for
building character for eternity is
in the nursery. The mother is queen
of that realm and sways a scepter more
potent than that of kings or priests.

185.

I long to put the experience of fifty years
at once into your young lives, to give you
at once the key of that treasure chamber
every gem of which has cost me tears and
struggles and prayers, but you must work
for these inward treasures yourselves.

Harriet Beecher Stowe

186.

For the mother is and must be, whether
she knows it or not, the greatest, strongest
and most lasting teacher her children have.

Hannah Whitall Smith

187.

My mother took for her motto in the training of her children the saying of some distinguished man: "Fill the measure with wheat and there will be no room for the chaff."

Maria Sandford

188.

All that I am my mother made me.

John Quincy Adams

189.

The mother's love is like God's love;
He loves us not because we are lovable,
but because it is His nature to love,
and because we are His children.

Earl Riney

190.

Giving advice comes naturally to mothers. Advice is in the genes along with blue eyes and red hair.

Lois Wyse

191.

Eventually your heart tells you
the best way to raise your children.

Steve Biddulph

192.

A mother has perhaps the hardest
earthly lot; and yet no mother worthy
of the name ever gave herself thoroughly
for her child who did not feel that, after
all, she reaped what she had sown.

Henry Ward Beecher

193.

Children cannot be made good
by making them happy, but
they can be made happy by
making them good.

E. J. Kiefer

194.

All that is purest and best in man is
but the echo of a mother's benediction.

Frederick W. Morton

195.

Happy is the child to whom the
love of a mother is a noble stimulus.

Hamilton Wright Mabie

196.

The mother's heart is
the child's schoolroom.

Henry Ward Beecher

197.

If you bend over backwards
for your children, you will
eventually lose your balance.

John Rosemond

198.

A mother is not a person to lean on, but a
person who makes leaning unnecessary.

Dorothy Fisher

199.

Judicious mothers always keep in mind
that they are the first book read, and
the last put aside, in every child's library.

C. Lenox Remond

200.

Being a mother enables
one to influence the future.

Jane Sellman

201.

Say to mothers what a
holy charge is theirs; with what
a kingly power their love might rule
the fountains of the newborn mind.

Lydia Huntley Sigourney

202.

The hand that rocks the cradle
is the hand that rules the world.

William Ross Wallace

203.

Listen to your father, who gave you life,
and do not despise your mother when she is
old. Buy the truth and do not sell it; get wisdom,
discipline and understanding. The father of a
righteous man has great joy; he who has a wise
son delights in him. May your father and mother
be glad; may she who gave you birth rejoice!

Proverbs 23:22-25

204.

Never fear spoiling children by making them too happy. Happiness is the atmosphere in which all good affections grow.

Charles Bray

205.

Who but a mother shares your moments of glory? Who else sees you at your weakest and most vulnerable and picks you up, helping you grow strong?
Your mom believes in your dreams, even when they lie in tatters at your feet. She picks you up and helps you dream again.

206.

My mother was the making of me.
She was so true, so sure of me;
and I felt I had something to live for,
someone I must not disappoint.

Thomas Edison

207.

These commandments that I give you today are to be upon your hearts. Impress them on your children. Talk about them when you sit at home and when you walk along the road, when you lie down and when you get up.

Deuteronomy 6:6-7

208.

To show a child what once delighted you, to find the child's delight added to your own, this is happiness.

J. B. Priestly

209.

Furnish an example, stop preaching, stop shielding, don't prevent self-reliance and initiative, allow your children to develop along their own lines.

Eleanor Roosevelt

210.

Young people say their number one source of
spiritual truth is Mom and Dad – not the church,
not the youth pastor or anyone else.

Josh McDowell

211.

It is better to
build strong children
than try to repair adults.

212.

The family should be a place where
each new human being can have an
early atmosphere conducive to the
development of constructive creativity.

Edith Schaeffer

A Mother's Duty

213.

Do not exasperate your
children; instead, bring
them up in the training and
instruction of the Lord.

Ephesians 6:4

214.

When you lead your sons
and daughters in the good way,
let your words be tender and
caressing, in terms of discipline
that wins the heart's assent.

Elijah Ben Solomon Zalman

215.

Let thy child's first
lesson be obedience,
and the second will
be what thou wilt.

Benjamin Franklin

216.

You can fool all of the people some
of the time, and some of the people all
of the time, but you can't fool Mom!

217.

Compassion will cure more
sins than condemnation.

Henry Ward Beecher

218.

It is much easier to fix
blame than to fix problems.

Kathleen Parker

219.

Consider carefully before you
say a hard word, but never let
a chance to say a good one go by.

George Horace Lorimer

220.

Be not angry that you cannot make
others as you wish them to be, since you
cannot make yourself as you wish to be.

Thomas à Kempis

236.

All who strive for reconciliation seek to listen rather than to convince, to understand rather than to impose themselves.

Brother Roger

237.

We ought to be much more tolerant about faulty behavior. We can all fall into one of Satan's traps here: it is so easy to give the impression of super holiness.

John Calvin

238.

Healthy parenting can be boiled down to two essential ingredients: love and control

James Dobson

239.

Discipline your son, for in that there is hope; do not be a willing party to his death.

Proverbs 19:18

232.

"Simply let your 'Yes' be
'Yes,' and your 'No,' 'No'".

Matthew 5:37

233.

Criticism, like rain, should be gentle
enough to nourish growth without
destroying the roots.

Frank A. Clark

234.

If a child lives with criticism, he learns
to condemn. If a child lives with hostility,
he learns to fight. If a child lives with
ridicule, he learns to be shy. If
a child lives with fairness, he learns justice.

Dorothy Nolte

235.

Forgiveness is the answer to the child's dream
of a miracle by which what is broken is made
whole again, what is soiled is again made clean.

Dag Hammarskjöld

227.

A refusal to correct is a refusal to love;
love your children by disciplining them.

Proverbs 13:24 THE MESSAGE

228.

To understand is not only
to pardon, but in the end to love.

Walter Lippmann

229.

Children can stand vast amounts of
sternness. It is injustice, inequity,
and inconsistency that kill them.

Robert Capon

230.

When you forgive, you in no way change the
past – but you sure do change the future.

Bernard Meltzer

231.

Discipline and love are not
opposites, one is a function of the other.

James Dobson

222.

He who covers over an
offense promotes love.

Proverbs 17:9

223.

Be aware that young people
have to be able to make their
own mistakes and that times change.

Gina Shapira

224.

He who does not punish
evil commands it to be done.

Leonardo da Vinci

225.

When a mother forgives, she kisses
the offense into everlasting forgetfulness.

226.

Re raising kids: Love, without discipline, isn't.

Malcolm Forbes

221.

The rod of correction imparts wisdom, but a child left to himself disgraces his mother.

Proverbs 29:15

Bonding

240.

Children are a gift from the LORD;
they are a reward from Him.

Psalm 127:3 NLT

241.

Many things we need can wait, children cannot.
Now is the time when their bones are being
formed; their blood is being made; their minds
are being developed. To them we cannot
say tomorrow; their name is today.

Gabriela Mistral

242.

Tolerance consists of seeing certain things
with your heart instead of with your eyes.

Orlando Battista

243.

Level with your children by being honest.
Nobody spots a phony quicker than a child.

Mary MacCracken

244.

The key to a loving relationship
between parent and child is this: You
don't love your children because of what
they do, but because of who they are.

245.

You can do anything with
children if you only play with them.

Otto van Bismarck

246.

You may be deceived if you trust
too much, but you will live in
torment if you do not trust enough.

Frank Crane

247.

For You created my inmost being; You knit me
together in my mother's womb. I praise You
because I am fearfully and wonderfully made;
Your works are wonderful, I know that full well.

Psalm 139:13-14

248.

Help your child to understand that
it is better to have one true friend than
all the acquaintances in the world.

249.

The thing most people want is genuine
understanding. If you can understand
the feelings and moods of another person,
you have something fine to offer.

Paul Brock

250.

If your children spend most of their time in
other people's houses, you're lucky; if they all
congregate at your house, you're blessed.

251.

The personal and daily contact between
mother and son have a sacramental virtue
in guarding and shaping a boy's course
such as nothing else on earth can supply.

G. W. E. Russell

252.

What heart like Mother's can forgive
the oft repeated wrongs of youth?
What hand like hers can lead us back
from sin to innocence and truth?

Caleb Dunn

253.

The best thing parents can spend
on their children is time, not money.

254.

Children are unpredictable.
You never know what inconsistency
they're going to catch you in next.

F. P. Jones

255.

One of life's pleasantest moments
comes when you don't have to pretend
any longer that you know everything.

256.

It is beyond a doubt that everyone should
have time for some special delight, if only
five minutes each day to seek out a
lovely flower or cloud or a star, or learn
a verse, or brighten another's dull task.

Helen Keller

257.

"Do to others as you would
have them do to you."

Luke 6:31

258.

Be humble and gentle. Be patient with
each other, making allowance for
each other's faults because of your love.

Ephesians 4:2 NLT

259.

People who really love each other are the
happiest people in the world. They love
their children and they love their families.
They may have very little … but they are happy.

Mother Teresa

260.

You can never establish a personal relationship
without opening up your own heart.

Paul Tournier

261.

Kind words are jewels that live in the heart
and soul and remain as blessed memories
years after they have been spoken.

Marvea Johnson

262.

The time to be happy is now.
The place to be happy is here. The way
to be happy is to make others so.

Robert Ingersoll

263.

Teach your child that it may take years
to win somebody's confidence, and
only a matter of seconds to lose it.

The Value of a Child

264.

Parents need to fill a child's bucket of
self-esteem so high that the rest of the world can't
poke enough holes to drain it dry.

Alvin Price

265.

The first and prime want in human nature
is the desire to be important.

John Dewey

266.

Tact is rubbing out another's
mistake instead of rubbing it in.

267.

We need, above all, to learn again to believe in
the possibility of nobility of spirit in ourselves.

Eugene O'Neill

268.

No one can make you feel inferior
without your consent.

Eleanor Roosevelt

269.

A person's attitude toward himself has a
profound influence on his attitude toward God,
his family, his friends, his future, and many
other significant areas of his life.

Bill Gothard

270.

In proportion to the development
of his individuality, each person
becomes more valuable to others.

John Stuart Mill

271.

Hide not your talents, they for use were
made. What's a sundial in the shade?

Benjamin Franklin

272.

If a man is unkind to himself, how can we
expect him to be compassionate to others?

Jewish proverb

273.

The deepest principle in human
nature is the craving to be appreciated.

William James

274.

First learn to love yourself,
then you can love me.

St. Bernard of Clairvaux

275.

How great is the love the Father has lavished
on us, that we should be called children
of God! And that is what we are!

1 John 3:1

276.

One of the greatest talents of all
is the talent to recognize
and to develop talent in others.

Frank Tyger

277.

It is how we perceive ourselves and
how these thought processes affect
our behavior that determines our
successes or failures in life.

John and Helen Boyle

278.

The confidence which we have
in ourselves gives birth to much of
that which we have in others.

Francois de la Rochefoucauld

279.

Use what talents you possess:
the woods would be very silent if no bird
sang there except those that sang best.

Henry van Dyke

280.

All true love is founded on esteem.

George Buckingham

281.

To improve the golden moments of opportunity and catch the good that is within our reach, is the great art of life.

Samuel Johnson

282.

We have different gifts, according to the grace given us.

Romans 12:6

283.

Treat people as if they were what they ought to be and you help them become what they are capable of being.

Johann Wolfgang von Goethe

284.

If a child lives with praise, he learns to be appreciative. If a child lives with acceptance, he learns to love.

285.

Abilities wither under faultfinding, blossom under encouragement.

Donald Laird

286.

The future belongs to those who believe in the beauty of their dreams.

Eleanor Roosevelt

287.

The art of using moderate abilities to advantage wins praise, and often acquires more reputation than actual brilliance.

Francois de la Rochefoucauld

288.

Therefore encourage one another and build each other up, just as in fact you are doing.

1 Thessalonians 5:11

289.

If a child lives with approval, he learns to like himself. If a child lives with recognition, he learns to have a goal.

290.

If we don't think we are worth much ourselves, surely our children won't think much of themselves either.

Cliff Shimmels

291.

God designed us to be tremendously productive and "to mount up with wings like eagles," realistically dreaming of what He can do with our potential.

Carol Kent

292.

Children are likely to become what their parents believe of them.

A Successful Life

293.

A successful life is not an easy life.
It is built upon strong qualities, sacrifice,
endeavor, loyalty, integrity.

Grant Brandon

294.

People rarely succeed unless they
have fun in what they are doing.

Dale Carnegie

295.

Encourage your children by reminding
them, "Your talent is God's gift to you. What
you do with it is your gift to God."

Leo Buscaglia

296.

Never mind what others do; do better
than yourself, beat your own record
from day to day, and you are a success.

William Boetcker

297.

Do a little more each day
than you think you possibly can.

Lowell Thomas

298.

By different methods different men excel,
but where is he who can do all things well?

Charles Churchill

299.

Failure doesn't mean you should give
up; it does mean you must try harder.

300.

When love and skill work
together, expect a masterpiece.

John Ruskin

301.

Excuses are the nails used to
build a house of failure.

302.

Let us recognize the beauty and power of true enthusiasm; and whatever we may do to enlighten ourselves or others, guard against checking or chilling a single earnest sentiment.

Henry Tuckerman

303.

Whether our efforts are, or not, favored by life, let us be able to say, when we come near to the great goal, I have done what I could.

Louis Pasteur

304.

He who stops being
better stops being good.

Oliver Cromwell

305.

If successful, don't crow;
if defeated, don't croak.

Samuel Chadwick

306.

If at first you don't succeed,
try, try and try again.

307.

Whatever your work is, dignify it
with your best thought and effort.

Esther Baldwin York

308.

Our prayers are answered not when we
are given what we ask, but when we
are challenged to be what we can be.

Morris Adler

309.

Perseverance is failing
19 times and succeeding the 20th.

J. Andrews

310.

A man can do his best only by confidently
seeking (and perpetually missing)
an unattainable perfection.

Ralph Barton Perry

311.

The greatest things ever done
on earth have been done little by little.

Thomas Guthrie

A Mother's Example

312.

A mother is the soil in
which her children grow.

Katherine Butler Hathaway

313.

The Golden Rule of Motherhood is:
"Tell me, and I'll forget. Show me,
and I may remember. Involve me,
and I will understand." And that
goes for your prayer life, too.
If you're not on your knees,
how could you expect your child to be?

Anne Graham Lotz

314.

Sit in the seat of thy mother,
and walk in thy mother's footsteps.

Johann Gottfried von Herder

315.

Character is formed, not by laws, commands, and decrees, but by quiet influence, unconscious suggestion, and personal guidance.

Marion L. Burton

316.

My mother had the greatest part in establishing the highest values of my life.

John Wesley

317.

What parent can tell when some fragmentary gift of knowledge or wisdom will enrich her children's lives?

Helena Rubenstein

318.

The most influential of all educational factors is the conversation in a child's home.

William Temple

319.

Children have never been very good
at listening to their elders, but they
have never failed to imitate them.

James Baldwin

320.

Follow my example,
as I follow the example of Christ.

1 Corinthians 11:1

321.

What we learn with
pleasure we never forget.

Louis Mercier

322.

The cry of many children to the adults in
their world is, "What you do speaks
so loud that I cannot hear what you say."

Millard Fuller

323.

He who makes no mistakes,
never makes anything.

English proverb

324.

Our walk counts far more
than our talk, always.

George Müller

325.

We unconsciously imitate what
pleases us, and approximate to
the characters we most admire.

Christian Bovée

326.

The first great gift we can bestow
on others is a good example.

Thomas Morell

327.

I regard no man as poor
who has a godly mother.

Abraham Lincoln

328.

Mothers who are able
to control and appropriately express
their own emotions, help their
children to develop emotional maturity.

329.

All our actions take their hue from
the complexion of the heart,
as landscapes their variety from light.

Francis Bacon

330.

A child's life is like a piece of paper on
which every passerby leaves a mark.

Chinese proverb

331.

In everything set them an example
by doing what is good. In your
teaching show integrity.

Titus 2:7

Motherhood

332.

Nothing will ever make you as happy or as sad,
as proud or as tired as motherhood.

Ella Parsons

333.

Every day look at a beautiful picture, read a
beautiful poem, listen to beautiful music,
and, if possible, say some reasonable thing.

Johann Wolfgang von Goethe

334.

Faithfulness in carrying our present duties
is the best preparation for the future.

Francois Fénelon

335.

Kindness is the sunshine
in which virtue grows.

Robert Green Ingersoll

336.

The loveliest masterpiece of the heart
of God is the heart of a mother.

Thérèse of Lisieux

337.

To be a mother is the grandest vocation
in the world. She holds in her
hands the destiny of nations.

Hannah Whitall Smith

338.

There is no higher height to
which humanity can attain than
that occupied by a devoted,
heaven-inspired, praying mother.

339.

A mother is kindness …
The sympathetic soul
of all existence.

Joyce Bark Russell

340.

God sends children to enlarge our hearts;
and to make us unselfish and full of kindly
sympathies and affections; to give our souls
higher aims; to call out all our faculties
to extended enterprise and exertion; and
to bring round our firesides bright faces,
happy smiles, and tender loving hearts.

Mary Howitt

341.

The Lord blesses the home of the righteous.

Proverbs 3:33

342.

What feeling is so nice as a child's hand
in yours? So small, so soft and warm, like a
kitten huddling in the shelter of your clasp.

Marjorie Holmes

343.

Some mothers never lose their beauty
even when they become old. They merely
shift it from their faces to their hearts.

344.

With every deed you are sowing a seed
though the harvest you may not see.

Ella Wheeler Wilcox

345.

The vocabulary of a mother's love
doesn't contain the word impossible.

Anne Paddock

346.

Blessed are the mothers of the earth.
They combine the practical and the spiritual
into the workable way of human life.

William Stinger

347.

Time spent with
children is never wasted.

348.

God's intimate friendship
blessed my house.

Job 29:4

349.

Some of the best things you can give
your children are good memories.

350.

Blessed be childhood which brings
down something of heaven into
the midst of our rough earthliness.

Henri Amiel

351.

Children are God's apostles sent forth day by
day to preach of love, and hope, and peace.

James Russell Lowell

352.

A mom's gift is always the best because it's
wrapped in love and tied up with heartstrings.

353.

All that is purest and best in man is
but the echo of a mother's benediction.

Frederick Morton

354.

One is happy once one knows the necessary ingredients of happiness – simple tastes, a certain degree of courage, self-denial to a point, love of work, and above all, a clear conscience. Let us live life as it is, and not be ungrateful.

George Sand

355.

My dear mother with the truthfulness of a mother's heart, ministered to all my woes, outward and inward, and even against hope kept prophesying good.

Thomas Carlyle

356.

Teach your children to brush their teeth, brush their hair and brush the dog, but not with the same brush. The dog resents it.

Peggy Goldtrap

357.

The way to make your children miserable is to satisfy all their desires.

358.

Sweet is the smile of home; the mutual look,
where hearts are of each other sure.

John Keble

359.

Being a mother enables
one to influence the future.

Jane Sellmam

360.

No dreamer is ever too small;
no dream is ever too big.

361.

The vision that you glorify in your mind, the
ideal that you enthrone in your heart – this you
will build your life by, this you will become.

James Allen

362.

You cannot teach a [child] anything.
You can only help him discover it within himself.

Galileo

363.

The best and most beautiful things
in life cannot be seen or touched.
They must be felt with the heart.

Helen Keller

364.

The only lasting happiness in life lies
in losing yourself in something that is
bigger, better, more lasting and of greater
worth than your own small existence.

Mother Teresa

365.

The song of the mothers! In infancy
our lullaby; in youth our high,
clear call to straightness of life;
in age our oftenest rehearsed refrain.

W. J. Cameron